KEVIN DURANT

Rise Above And Shoot
The Kevin Durant Story

WHAT IT TAKES TO BE LIKE DURANT

An Unauthorized Biography

By Steve James

"Hard work beats talent when talent fails to work hard."

- Kevin Durant

TABLE OF CONTENTS

INTRODUCTION

When *Kevin Durant won the MVP in 2014* he delivered one of the most emotional and captivating speeches in basketball history. Holding back tears throughout, and letting some go, he thanked his teammates and his family sincerely, for helping him reach the level of success that he has obtained.

Some criticized Durant, for letting the tears run down his face, but others commended him for exuding a genuine demeanor that few people are capable of expressing. Kevin Durant is truly a grateful person.

Durant grew up with little promise in his life; he was born to a young single mother in a poor area of Maryland. Nothing would be handed to him, and nothing was. Aside from being blessed with a 5-inch growth spurt in high school and a 6'9" frame, Durant has worked through sweat and blood to arrive where he is today, and he is still not yet satisfied.

This book will take us through Durant's life from his hometown in Maryland, to his year at Texas, to his career in Oklahoma City, and everywhere he has gone in between. It will show us where he struggled, and where he excelled. We will learn about his personal life and how he has developed the mentality that he has today. What does he eat? What kind of drills does he do? How does he develop his innovative ways of scoring? **What makes him one of the most amazing players to watch?**

This book answers these questions and more. In addition to his training techniques we will learn about his mental preparation, including what he does off the court. Durant has a life outside of basketball; he enjoys playing video games with childhood friends, he is starting business ventures, and giving back to the community. We'll even discuss his superstitions and intricacies.

The book is an in-depth and comprehensive perspective on one of

the greatest scorers of all time and one of the most promising athletes of a generation. Everyone that reads this book will come away with something different, but everyone will come away with something substantial.

CHAPTER 1

THE EARLY YEARS

On September 29, 1988, Wanda Pratt gave birth to Kevin Wayne Durant in Washington D.C. Before Durant reached the age of one, his father left the family. Pratt and her mother, Barbara Davis, raised Kevin and his older brother Tony in Seat Pleasant, Maryland, in these formative years.

Durant and his brother grew up playing sports and were actively engaged in programs at the Boys & Girls club. Living in the Washington D.C. area, they were fans of the local sports teams. Durant closely followed the Washington Wizards at the time that Michael Jordan was on the team.

Durant was always unusually tall to the point where **he was often embarrassed of his height**. His lanky frame and his horizontal presence caused him to stand out, making him uncomfortable. His grandmother, a formative figure in his life, told him it would play to his advantage. And although he couldn't see it then, she would turn out to be correct.

At the young age of 11, Durant's potential and talent was already beginning to be realized. He played basketball for the Prince George Jaguars, a program with AAU teams for all ages. His team made it to the national championship game and he scored 18 points in the second half to win. It was then that *he made the declaration to his mother that he would be a professional basketball player in the*

NBA one day.

Also Jaguars were Michael Beasley and Chris Braswell (current professional basketball players for teams in China and Europe, respectively). Beasley and Durant were sons of two single mothers at the time, and in order to lighten each other's loads, the mother's frequently took care of the boys to help out. Most mornings Beasley would be dropped off at Durant's house for breakfast, and the two would ride the bus to school together.

When Durant said that he wanted to be a professional basketball player, **his mother, Wanda, played a big role** in developing not just Durant's physical prowess, but also his mental edge. She would do crazy things like wake him up in the middle of the night and have him do up to 100 pushups, or tell him to do sprints up and down the stairs. When she attended his practices growing up she encouraged his coaches to push her son harder than they already were. More than just basketball, Wanda saw Durant's interest in basketball as an opportunity for him not to just develop as a player, but also to develop as a person. It was a way to keep him off the streets, learn the importance of discipline, and push himself to new levels.

Durant's father, Wayne Pratt, came back to the family when Durant was around 13 years old. He worked for the Library of Congress in Washington D.C., while his mother, Wanda, worked as a postal employee.

In 2003, the Jaguars ceased to exist and Durant took his talents to the DC Blue Devils. Tyson Lawson was Durant's teammate, a future ACC Player of the Year, and the boys were coached by Taras "Stink" Brown. Brown developed a long-term plan for Durant to achieve the highest level of success. In this plan he included Durant's exclusion from pickup games because Brown believed that could would bring about bad habits and cause potential injuries.

Instead, Durant was to follow a specific and orchestrated training regimen, which he took very seriously. During the summer, he had various drills, which he was supposed to perform on his own, and he did so religiously, often practicing up to eight hours every day. This **work ethic that Durant developed at such a young age, never dissipated**, and is what has led him to such a successful career.

CHAPTER 2

HIGH SCHOOL YEARS

Durant ended up going to Montrose Christian High School in Rockville, Maryland. Even in the 9th and 10th grades, Durant was already a name to watch out for on <u>the varsity team</u>. In his first year he encountered some problems – the older players, perhaps due to jealousy, threatened to stop passing him the ball. The following year he was **named the Player of the Year by** *The Washington Post.*

Of course, a massive growth spurt would be very beneficial to Durant in his high school years. <u>Between the freshman and sophomore season</u> he grew five inches. Already a tall young man at 6'3", growing to 6'8" made him quite the *anomaly*. Having done drills and training geared toward guards, Durant's new growth spurt enabled him to be a **rare forward who could both handle the ball and shoot from the outside**, as well as gave him a new skill set to work on.

While at Montrose Christian High School, **Durant developed his shot**. His coach, Stu Vetter, would have his players do form shooting without a ball, just to make the form feel as natural as possible. They would bend their knees, and fake a shot with a single hand. By eliminating their non-dominant guide hand, the drill emphasizes the straightness of what shots should be like.

After doing stationary shooting form, Vetter would make Durant and his other athletes step in to catch a fake ball, then proceed to a shot. Finally, the players would add the ball to the drill, taking short-range jump shots, and exaggerating the follow-through. They did these drills every day at the beginning of practice.

For his <u>junior year</u>, Durant transferred to Oak Hill Academy, where Lawson was already playing. This school, a Baptist school in Virginia, is well known for having a standout basketball program and has given opportunities to players like Carmelo Anthony, Stephen Jackson, Rajon Rondo, and many others.

The position at Oak Hill Academy was one with a lot of promise. Durant delivered a tremendous performance in his first year, averaging 19.6 points and getting 8.8 rebounds. His performances awarded him a **Second Team All-American position by *Parade Magazine***.

Despite the success, he moved yet again to the National Christian Academy for <u>his final year</u> with coach, Stu Vetter. He finished off his high school career scoring 23.6 points and getting 10.9 rebounds per game. He participated in the **McDonald's All-American game and was recognized as the co-MVP of the game**.

CHAPTER 3

NCAA – THE LONGHORN YEAR

Durant was scouted by nearly every top program in the country. A unique player at 6'9", with the skills and finesse of a point guard and the height and abilities of a forward, he was a potential future scoring threat. To put it simply, **he was on a different level than most other high school players**.

Former teammate, Lawson, wanted Durant to join him at the University of North Carolina, but a man by the name of Russell Springmann had been informally talking to Durant since his first year in high school. Springmann was an assistant at the University of Texas, and persuaded Durant to join him and become a Longhorn.

The summer before heading to Texas Durant tried to bulk up and become stronger. When he began the school year he was brought on as a starter. It only took a few months into the season for Durant to gain national acclaim as **many considered him the best player in the league**.

During the season he averaged about 26 points and 11 rebounds per games. On 20 separate occasions he had 30-point performances, and racking up 390 total rebounds put him as **third on the list of most rebounds by any freshman in NCAA history**.

Texas finished the season with a record of 25-10. They finished third in the Big 12 and ended up losing to Kansas in the final game of the Big 12 championship. Ultimately, the Longhorns received a Top 20 national ranking.

They were seeded fourth in the East Regional of the NCAA tournament. After winning the first round game by nearly 20 points over New Mexico State, they lost in an upset to USC in the next round. That season, Durant was named the *AP College Player of the Year* and he won the Naismith and Wooden awards.

It was obvious to almost everyone at this point that Durant would declare for the NBA draft. He did a few weeks later, as did Greg Oden, the other majorly discussed NCAA player from Ohio State.

Even though he only played at UT for one year, the school retired his jersey in 2009. His #35 stands up there along with T.J. Ford's #11 and Slater Martin's #15.

Durant's Strength Training Routine

Although Durant was only in college for a year, he took advantage of the training facilities and materials on site, and really became a much stronger player. A lot of his strength training was geared to increase mobility in his spine, hips and feet. Here are some of the exercises he did regularly:

Thoracic Spine Extension

- Position body inside Tru Stretch Cage or under reachable pull-up bar
- Grab top bar with right hand and stabilize body with left hand on side of structure
- Keeping hips even and without leaning excessively to one side, allow spine to extend into stretch

Reps/Duration: Hold 2x30 seconds each side

Rotational Med Ball Throws

- Assume athletic stance with wall to left; hold med ball in front
- Rotate right slightly to load right leg and hip
- Explode to left, rotating hips to throw ball at wall as hard as possible
- Repeat for specified reps
- Perform set on opposite side

Sets/Reps: 3x8 each side

Split-Stance Overhead Core Matrix

Forward

- Assume split stance with cable machine behind
- Hold cable attachment above head and lean forward slightly to create stretch through abdominal region
- Shift hips back and drive torso forward until it is parallel to ground
- Return to start position with control and repeat for specified reps
- Perform set with opposite leg forward

Rotational

- Assume split stance with right leg forward and cable machine behind
- Hold cable attachment above right shoulder and lean forward slightly to create stretch and rotation through abdominal region
- Shift hips back and drive torso forward until it is parallel to ground
- Return to start position with control and repeat for specified reps
- Perform set with left leg forward starting over left shoulder

Lateral

- Assume athletic stance with cable machine to left and hold cable attachment above head
- Shift hips left and drive torso right
- Return to start position with control and repeat for specified reps
- Perform set with cable machine to right

Sets/Reps: 2x10 each variation

Med Ball Multi-Planar Lunge on Core Board

- Assume athletic stance holding med ball in front
- Keeping shoulders facing straight ahead, step forward and 45 degrees left onto Core Board with right leg
- Lower into crossover lunge position until back knee is just above floor
- Drive back off right heel into start position
- Perform lunge straight ahead onto Core Board with right leg; return to start position
- Perform lunge forward and 45 degrees right onto Core Board with right leg, return to start position
- Repeat sequence for specified reps
- Perform set with left leg

Sets/Reps: 2-4x9-12 each leg [3-4 lunges in each position]

Coaching Points: Keep lunging knee behind toes (Draw stomach in throughout set). Keep shoulders straight ahead, not in direction you're stepping.

Daub: I keep my hand on Kevin's knee to make sure there is no [forward] shifting, which can put undue stress on the knee. We do a lot of multi-planar movements to place him in a very difficult situation as far as his knee, hip and back alignment is concerned. This trains him to pull himself out of a position like that when he gets knocked off balance in a game. It's all about strengthening within the different planes that he's going to be involved with in basketball. This trains the true core–rather than just doing an ab exercise like a sit-up.

Basic Med Ball Multi-Planar Lunge

Perform same exercise as above without the Core Boards.

Stein: This is used to vary the normal front-to-back range of motion as well as strengthen the muscles of the groin and hips.

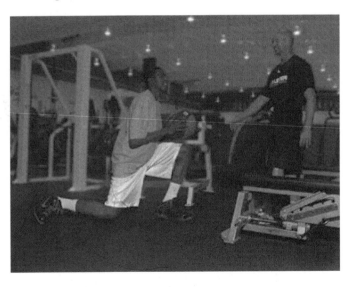

Three-Way Med Ball Single-Leg Romanian Deadlift on Airex Pad

- Standing on one leg on Airex Pad, hold med ball in front
- Keeping back flat, shoulder blades together and balancing leg slightly bent, fold at waist and bring med ball toward one of three cones set up in front of you
- Return to start position; perform movement to each of the other two cones
- Repeat for specified reps
- Perform set on opposite leg

Sets/Reps: 2-4x5-7 each leg

Coaching Points: Keep back flat. Don't allow knee to shift forward. Keep back leg straight behind you.

Daub This isolates the hamstring and glute because of the stabilization factor. It's also a tremendous exercise for ankle stabilization when you introduce the Airex Pad.

Basic Med Ball Single-Leg Romanian Deadlift

Perform same exercise as above with foot on flat ground.

Stein: This strengthens the back side of the body and works the stabilizing muscles, tendons and ligaments of the ankle, knee and hip.

Single-Leg Dumbbell Curl-to-Press

- Balance on one leg, holding dumbbells at sides with palms facing forward
- Curl dumbbells to shoulders, then press them straight overhead as you rotate palms to face out
- Slowly lower dumbbells to start position through same movement pattern
- Repeat for specified reps

Sets/Reps: 3x4-6-8 [switch legs halfway through each set]

Coaching Points: Keep balancing knee slightly bent. Don't swing dumbbells. Don't overarch back during press.

Daub: This is great for single-leg proprioception and balance. It is a combo lift because it's a Bicep Curl associated with a Shoulder Press. Combo exercises allow us to get our training done in less time and also to put Kevin in a position where he has to stabilize with his core to go through the different movements.

Basic Dumbbell Overhead Press

Perform Press with dumbbells while standing on both feet.

Stein: This strengthens the shoulders and core. I prefer to use the standing position to involve all of the body's stabilizing muscles.

Inverted Row on Physioball with TRX Straps

- Hold onto straps, then place heels on top of physioball making sure body is in straight line

- Keeping body rigid, pull body up until chest is even with hands

- Lower with control until arms are straight

- Repeat for specified reps

Sets/Reps: 3-4x6-10

Coaching Points: Equally distribute weight with feet on ball. Keep body straight with no sag in hips. Get full extension with arms at bottom of movement.

Daub: The ball adds another dimension that makes it more difficult. It becomes a core exercise because he has to stabilize his entire body in a straight line, and he is still getting the rowing effect of the exercise.

Basic Inverted Row

Perform same exercise holding onto barbell with feet on ground

Stein: This strengthens the posterior side of the body and is a nice alternative for players who have difficulty doing standard pull-ups.

Walking Dumbbell Push-Up-to-Row

- Assume push-up position with light dumbbells in hands and legs slightly wider than hip width

- Walk left dumbbell forward a few inches, then right dumbbell while dragging legs forward

- Perform push-up

- Perform row with left arm, then right

- Repeat sequence [walk, walk, push-up, row, row] for specified reps

Sets/Reps: 2-4x3-8 [entire sequence constitutes one rep]

Coaching Points: Keep opposite arm locked out during row. Keep body in straight line. Keep feet wide to help balance.

Daub: This is a tremendous combination exercise that trains the entire upper body. You use your shoulders, lats, chest and core for stabilization. The reps depend on the strength level of the athlete.

Basic Dumbbell Row From Push-Up Position

Perform rows in alternating fashion without walking the dumbbells forward or performing push-ups.

Stein: This is a tremendous exercise when you have limited equipment. It strengthens all muscles of the upper body.

CHAPTER 4

PROFESSIONAL NBA CAREER

DRAFT

Greg Oden and Kevin Durant had been the two most-talked about NCAA players the year they entered the draft and many wondered which one would be the first overall draft pick. Ultimately, the Portland Trailblazers, who had the first pick that year, would go with Oden. **Durant was the second draft selection**, and headed to Seattle to play for the Supersonics.

2007-2008 Season

In the season opener against the Denver Nuggets, Durant scored 18 points, got 5 rebounds, and grabbed 3 steals, although his team lost the game. Just a few weeks later, on November 16, Seattle squared off against the Atlanta Hawks. Durant made his first-ever game winning shot. Although the Sonics only won 20 games, Durant finished off the season with averages of 20.3 points, 4.4 rebounds, 2.4 assists, and 1 steal per game, joining the ranks of Carmelo Anthony and LeBron James as being the only teenagers to average over 20 points a game in NBA history. His first-year performances earned him the title of *Rookie of the Year*, the first ever Supersonic to do so.

A lot was up in the air for the Sonics the following year. Owner, Clay Bennett, was not able to lobby to get enough money for a new arena in Seattle. Thus, **the team was relocated to Oklahoma City and named the Thunder**. Along with Durant and fellow rookie Jeff Green, the two moved to Oklahoma City to begin their second NBA season with Russell Westbrook.

2008-2009 Season

The following year definitely saw improvement, although perhaps not might as much as they had hoped for. After a nine-game winning streak the Thunder were able to win 50 games. In the process they were able to blow out some of the best teams – the Orlando Magic, the Los Angeles Lakers – and won games playing away against the Celtics and the Spurs, which is no easy feat.

During the 2009 NBA All-Star Weekend Durant participated in the *Rookie Challenge game* – a competition set up for first and second year players. He scored 46 points in the game. Additionally, his yearly averages increased to 25.3 points and 7 rebounds per game, shooing 47.7% from the field. Finally, he came in third in the voting for the Most Improved Player Award.

2009-2010 Season

Heading into the 2009-2010 season, people certainly expected big things from Durant. And he certainly delivered. Not only would he end up averaging over 30 points per game, but also he helped the Thunder to add 27 wins to their record the next year. His yearly averages made him **the youngest player in NBA history to be the scoring champion of the season.**

In his first-ever playoff game, he scored 24 points against the Los Angeles Lakers, although the Thunder lost the game. Ultimately, the Lakers beat the Thunder in six games. But the team's massive improvement put them on the radar as a serious future threat.

Throughout the season Durant hit a number of milestones. He scored over 25 points in 29 consecutive games, setting a franchise record. He also scored over 30 points in seven consecutive games. And finally, he scored over 40 points in three consecutive games. Only 21 years old when the season finished and with 2,472, and having outscored LeBron James, Durant became the youngest player in NBA history to win the overall scoring title. Additionally, he was *selected to the All-Star game* for the first time, and also made his first All-NBA team.

2010-2011 Season

Durant signed a five-year contract extension for $86 million heading into the 2010-2011 season. The following years were considered to be "building years" and Oklahoma City was not seen as a team was likely to begin contending for a title. After averaging 27.7 points per game during the season, again **leading the NBA in points**, the Thunder acquired the 4th seed in the playoffs with 55 wins.

The Thunder came out strong, and slid past the Denver Nuggets in the first round. It was a hard-fought first round win, despite the fact that the Thunder won the three of the first four games. In Game 5 it looked as though the Nuggets might be able to win, but with Durant scored 16 points in the last 12 minutes of the game, scoring 41 points, and Oklahoma City came out with a win.

The second round they faced the Memphis Grizzlies. Memphis squeezed out the series to seven games, but the Thunder ended up winning it and made it to the Conference Finals to play the Dallas Mavericks. Ultimately, they lost to the Mavericks in five games, but they saw significant improvement from the previous year.

2011-2012 Season

During the off-season over the summer, Durant was said to be putting in countless hours of work with his trainer, Justin Zormelo. Reports said that he was beginning workouts at 6 in the morning and not finishing until the evening. Although the season was shorter because of the lockout, Oklahoma City came out on fire.

James Harden and Serge Ibaka added to a deep starting lineup, but Durant's scoring did not cease. In February, he scored a career-high 51 points. In the All-Star Game, he also scored 36 points to help the West beat the East 152-149. The performance earned him the *All-Star Game MVP Award*.

The Thunder won 47 games and earned the second seed heading into the playoffs. They were matched up against Dallas, the team who had knocked them out the previous year. Durant hit a game-winning shot with less than two seconds in the game to win Game 1. They progressed smoothly, beating Dallas, the Lakers, the Spurs, and Durant made it to his first NBA championship series against the Miami Heat.

Despite some unbelievable performances, the Heat won the series. Durant had the highest scoring averages for both teams, at 30.6 points per game, shooting 54.8% from the field. However, it was not enough to beat LeBron James, Dwayne Wade, Chris Bosh, and the Miami supporting cast.

2012-2013 Season

After losing the championship, Durant put in a lot of hard work over the summer and came back to average 28.1 points per game in the next season. Although he did not achieve the credibility of the highest scorer again, he shot *51% from the field* and *41.6% from behind the arc*. Most notably, perhaps, he shot *over 90% from the free throw line*.

The Thunder finished the season with a 60-22 record and became the first seed going into the playoffs. In the first series, the Thunder faced the Houston Rockets. Unfortunately, Russell Westbrook tore his meniscus early on, and although the Thunder were able to win the first series, they fell to the Memphis Grizzlies in the second round. Durant stepped up averaging 30.8 points per game in the post season, but it was not enough to get Oklahoma City past the second round.

2013-2014 Season

The 2013-2014 season was a **banner year for Durant**. He scored over 30 points in 12 consecutive games. In January, he was on fire, averaging almost 36 points per game, including a career-high performance scoring 54 points against the Golden State Warriors. His final season averages – 32 points, 7.4 rebounds, and 5.5 assists per game, were considered universally impressive, and were enough to win him the *Most Valuable Player* award.

Despite this amazing season, when the playoffs rolled around Durant was inconsistent. The Thunder fell behind the Grizzlies in the first round 3-2. Unsure whether or not they would be able to pull off the win, the local newspaper, *The Oklahoman*, referred to him as "*Mr. Unreliable.*" However, he bounced back in the next game, making a statement by scoring 36 points. They beat the Grizzlies, and then surpassed the Los Angeles Clippers in the second round. However, they could not get past the Spurs in the Conference finals.

In Durant's MVP acceptance speech, he delivered emotional thanks to people close to him, especially his family. He shed tears throughout the speech and received a warm and strong reception. He talked about a rough upbringing, saying:

"Me, my mom, my brother – we moved so many different places growing up, and it felt like a box, it felt like there was no getting out. I've been through the toughest times with my family, but I'm still standing."

He also pointed out all of the players on his team, personally and dutifully. At the end of his speech as he thanked his mom, he concluded with, "*You're the real MVP.*"

2014-2015 Season

After the 2013-2014 season Durant spent most of the summer in Los Angeles, training harder than he had before. After a successful summer, as soon as the preseason practices began, **Durant fell to injury**. He was diagnosed with a Jones fracture, a stress fracture, in his right foot and was told to rest for 6-8 weeks.

He returned to the court on December 2, after having to sit out the first 17 games of the season. However, just a mere two weeks later, in a game against the Golden State Warriors, Durant injured his ankle.

Returning strong again shortly after, Durant scored 44 points against the Phoenix Suns on December 31. But less than a month later, he was sidelined again, spraining his left big toe. Finally, on February 22, he underwent a minor procedure in his foot, which translated into a larger foot surgery in the spring. Despite only playing 27 games in his injury-ridden 2014-2015 season, Durant averaged 25.4 points, 6.6 rebounds, and 4.1 assists per game.

2015-2016 Season

Having not gotten much court time in 2014-2015, Durant has returned in 2015 with a bang. On October 30, 2015, *he and Russell Westbrook became the first teammates to each score over 40 points in a game since the epic duo Michael Jordan and Scottie Pippen* (which occurred in 1996). Granted, this came in the form of a double-overtime win over the Orlando Magic. The final score was 139-136. Although he had to sit out for a week in November, he returned and has been delivering high-scoring performances since then.

CHAPTER 5

INTERNATIONAL BASKETBALL

In 2007, Durant was given an opportunity to try out for Team USA. However, Coach Mike Krzyzewski did not think Durant made the cut, mostly due to lack of experience. Durant finally made a national team in 2010 for the FIBA World Championship.

He helped lead Team USA to the World Championship title, which was the first title since 1994. He averaged 22.8 points, 6.1 rebounds, 3.1 assists, and 1.4 steals per game. The performances earned him **the title of MVP**.

He also travelled to London to compete in the 2012 Olympics. After scoring 19.5 points, getting 5.8 rebounds, dishing out 2.6 assists, and grabbing 1.6 steals per game, he was a critical part of the championship team. This included a 30-point game in the final which helped him to set the record for total points scored in an Olympic tournament.

CHAPTER 6

EXCLUSIVE DRILLS AND EXERCISES USED BY KEVIN DURANT

"I know that hard work got me here.
And the day I stop working hard,
this can all go away."
– Kevin Durant

We'll get more into Durant's mental edge later on, but it's important to note, that this lanky, young professional from Washington D.C. has had little handed to him in his life. While being 6'9" certainly helps, **Durant's work ethic is nearly unmatched by anyone in the world**. His training is both on and off the court, and it is extensive and critical to his achievements. Here is an inside look as some of this training.

A word about his diet

Durant is a noticeably thin player. This is in part because of his general build; he's tall, 6'9" and weighs a reported 240 pounds. But that said, he is still leaner then most players. While some critics have said that Durant would need to gain weight to be a serious competitor in the league, he has given up any plans to gain weight.

However, looking at photographs throughout Durant's life, it is evident that he is naturally a lean guy. Thus, instead of trying to artificially bulk up, Durant tries to stick to a healthy diet, high in proteins and vegetables, which will give him high energy throughout a game.

He often eats oatmeal with fruit for breakfast and protein bars (SNACK and KIND) for snacks throughout the day. His frequent pregame meal is fish and vegetables. A postgame or workout meal will be a bit heavier, like steak or chicken and rice. He is also a fan of fried chicken, snack food, and of course, candy, but does his best to refrain as much as possible. At this point, a significant weight gain could force him to alter his game to a large degree, and actually make him a less effective player.

Off-Court Workouts

Sand Dune Workout

During summer training in Los Angeles Durant does a really interesting drill on sand dunes. A coach will put high cones in a line up the dune. Durant will run up the dune in only socks zigzagging through the cones. Then he'll do the same drill back pedaling. And finally, he will do side sliding, to emulate defensive play, but make it much more tiresome on the muscles.

Ropes

Like many basketball players, Durant uses ropes for strength and strength/endurance training. He'll take the heavy ropes in both arms and do a series of exercises with them, throwing them up and down simultaneously, alternating arms, etc.

On-Court Workouts

Long Walk to Shoot

This drill is a shooting drill, which looks a bit awkward. Durant will take long, lunge-like steps across the top of the key. Then he'll receive a pass on the opposite side before quickly squaring up and receiving the pass.

The Kevin Durant shooting workout is a great workout because it incorporates shooting, ball handling, footwork, and finishing drills that you will use in game-like situations.

Resistance Two-Ball Dribbling

Durant will take two balls and walk up and down the court asserting powerful and simultaneous dribbles into the ground. Throughout the duration of the drill, a teammate or trainer will put his hands on Durant's shoulders, causing resistance and making the training more difficult.

Physicality Driving Drill

In order to emulate some of the physical play that all players face, but especially that Durant faces, he does a physical double-team driving drill with two defenders. He runs to an elbow and receives a pass from the top of the key. Then two defenders will collapse on him, often deliberately fouling him, and he'll have to take on dribble and make it to the hoop. After averaging the amount of points that he has in recent years, he has to contend with physical double-teaming often.

2-Dribble Pull Up Drill

In this drill Durant takes a few dribbles from half court to the top of the key. Then he does a quick stutter step to shake the defense, and pulls up for a jump shot. He'll repeat numerous times.

Attack Help Defender

In this drill Durant is positioned at the top of the key. He goes to one side and then cuts across the middle of the court as if he is receiving an off-ball screen. He receives a pass on the opposite elbow and takes an explosive dribble before pulling up for a jump shot.

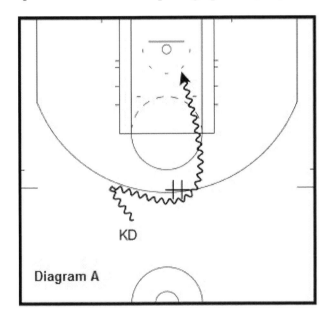

Diagram A

Dribble to Drag Crossover

This drill is structured to work on Durant's change of direction and explosiveness. Starting on a wing he'll take a few dribbles to the center, then pull a quick crossover and drive baseline for a dunk or a pull up jump shot.

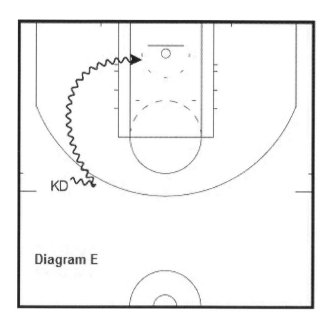

Diagram E

CHAPTER 7

PERSONAL LIFE, BUSINESS AND PHILANTHROPY

Personal Life

Although not from the Oklahoma City area, Durant has truly taken the city, which looks up to him so highly, to be his own. Throughout his years living there he has told numerous reporters how much he loves the place, which is not seen as a very desirable city in comparison to the rest of the cities in the United States, and how he feels obliged to go good for the city.

During the NBA Lockout Durant tweeted, *"This lockout is really boring..anybody playing flag football in Okc..I need to run around or something!"* An Oklahoma State University student responded telling Durant that his team was playing that evening. Durant asked, *"Can I play?"* and the student told him yes, but to bring is "A" Game.

Hundreds came out to watch the game, as he played and towered over everyone else. Afterwards Durant tweeted, "I had soooo much fun at Oklahoma st playing flag football! Shoutout my new buddy @groverbey for inviting me! I threw 4 tds and had 3 ints!!" Actions like these have made Durant **the beloved figure he is in Oklahoma City**.

Durant has often been talked about as **the most well-liked player in the game.** Various polls indicate that fans prefer Durant's personality over Kobe Bryant's and LeBron James. He has been dubbed, after a series of Foot Locker commercials ran in 2013, as the *"nicest guy in the NBA."* Thunder staff, too, have indicated that he is a humble and caring person.

For a period of time Durant was engaged to Monica Wright, a WNBA player. However, the two broke off the engagement in 2014. In Durant's nice character, he did not speak ill of her. In an interview with GQ he said:

"I had a fiancée, but...I really didn't know how to, like, love her, you know what I'm saying? We just went our separate ways. We were just hanging out, chilling. And I felt the energy. I felt, I need to do this right now. And I just did it. I was like...We're engaged right now? We're about to get married? So I was just like, cool! I love this girl. But I didn't love her the right way."

Some rumors have indicated that the reason for religious motives; more specifically, that Durant did not share her Christian faith. However, Durant is a practicing Christian, and attends chapel services before games. He also has religious tattoos on his body – stomach, back, and wrist.

Finally, Durant still remains very close friends with the people he grew up with. Not only has he financially supported many of his friends, and helped them move out to Oklahoma City, but when he is not playing basketball, he is hanging out with his childhood friends, playing video games and having a good time.

Business and Philanthropy

Durant owns a home in the Club Villa neighborhood, which he bought for $1.95 million in 2013. He also owns a restaurant called KD's Southern Cuisine in the neighborhood of Bricktown in the city. The restaurant is fairly flashy, although affordable, and offers up southern delicacies for all of the locals to enjoy.

Fans have been quoted in interviews citing Durant's friendly nature. Because Oklahoma City is relatively small, and Durant is quite noticeable, he is often seen milling about when he is not practicing. However, unlike many celebrities, he is always willing to engage with fans and locals. He's not dismissive, and will gladly have a conversation with people around town.

After the 2013 Moore tornado, which struck Oklahoma and killed 24 people while injuring 377 others, Durant quickly, and quietly, donated $1 million to the American Red Cross. Although he did not promote the fact that he did this, word spread, and the Thunder, as well as his sponsor, Nike, matched the donation, making a significant difference to the victims.

What many don't know is that **Durant resigned with Nike** after being offered more money elsewhere. Adidas offered Durant a 7-year deal for $70 million, which also included a $12 million signing bonus. However, he chose to sign again with Nike for over $12 million less. Few athletes uphold loyalty to a brand over such a large sum of money.

Durant also loves music, and **hopes to dedicate his life after basketball to the music world**. He is a spokesperson for the Washington D.C. branch of P'Tones Records. This national non-profit provides after school programs and recording opportunities for underprivileged youth.

Additionally, Durant is now represented by Jay-Z. His former agents were Aaron Goodwin and Rob Pelinka, but in 2013 he signed with the Roc Nation group, as he hopes to contribute to the music world as well.

Durant has partnerships with Nike, Sprint, Panini, General Electric, Gatorade, and 2K Sports. He made $35 million in 2013, making him one of the highest-earning athletes of the year. He has also emphasized his nice image by partnering with KIND snacks with advertisements saying things like *"Being kinds is not a sign of weakness."*

Finally, **Kevin Durant, himself, is a brand**. Not only does he have a massive shoe deal with Nike, but also there are lots of clothing with his initials. The KD shoes have sold well, and are seen in a range of bright enticing colors.

CHAPTER 8

HIS FEARS AND SUPERSTITIONS

Fears

Durant does not have any fears when it comes to physicality, wanting to try new moves, etc. Rather, his fears are much more deeply rooted. In an interview he brought this to light:

"My biggest fear is that I might be taking it all for granted. Being able to do something I love every single day is a blessing. We play so many games, we have so many practices - it flies by. By the time it's all said and done, I worry that I might not have really enjoyed every single day as a pro."

Superstitions

Although Durant does not have a long laundry list of superstitions and fears, he is known for having one specific superstition: he cannot watch important free throws.

When Russell Westbrook was on the line with less than 7 seconds left in a playoff game, Durant turned his back and squatted down. He explained that he doesn't not trust his teammates, but rather, he thinks he is bad luck to the team.

He also has said that every time he goes to a Redskins game or watches a Texas game, the Thunder loses. Thus, when he thinks it's going to be an issue, he simply turns his head.

Why Does Kevin Durant Wear #35?

The number on Durant's jersey carries significant meaning. He pays homage by wearing the number of years his first basketball coach, Charles Craig, had lived, when he was murdered in 2005. Craig was known to most as "Big Chucky" and was a formative person in Durant's life, teaching him basketball fundamentals, as well as life lessons. Growing up for many years without a father, he served such a role to Durant in his early life, but unfortunately was killed at 35.

CHAPTER 9

TOP 10 MOTIVATIONAL LESSONS FROM KEVIN DURANT

1. Never Settle for Second

Durant frequently alludes to his frustration with coming in second time and time again. He claims he was the second best player on his high school team (although that is debatable), he was the second pick in the NBA draft, and he has come in second in the NBA finals. Despite the fact that Durant has already accomplished a great deal in his career and despite the fact that many would already believe he's achieved great success, he remains thoroughly dissatisfied with his runner-up position, and wants to be a champion.

2. Enlist Support from People Around You

Durant has a close circle of friends and family whom have supported him for years. First and foremost is his mother, and his childhood friends follow not far behind. These people have been critical to Durant's success. Not only does he obtain motivation from wanting to make them proud of him, but also he is motivated to please them because of the ways in which they have invested time in his life.

3. Remember Where You Came From

In the same vain as the previous motivational lesson, Durant has never forgotten where he was raised and how it made him the person he is today. He frequently goes back to his hometown of Seat Pleasant and participates in pickup games and participates in a variety of events in the neighborhood. It is a humbling experience for him and he enjoys both inspiring young athletes and being inspired by children in a similar situation that he was when he was younger.

4. Give Back

As noted above, Durant continuously gives back to both the communities where he grew up, as well as the community of Oklahoma City. This extends beyond the camps with small children that he participates in. By opening up a restaurant in Oklahoma City, he is trying to actually add to the economy of the city. This is further evident by the fact that he quietly donated $1 million to the Red Cross after the devastating tornado in Moore.

5. Work Harder Every Time

The better Durant gets, the harder he seems to work. After losing in the NBA Finals, Durant could not even be convinced to take a week of rest. He was so motivated to be on top he went right into a summer of rigorous training. Even though he is considered one of the best players in the league his continuous work ethic makes it so that there is always something to improve upon.

6. Be Humble

Often cited as the nicest guy in the NBA, Durant is well known to be more humble than most superstars. He has a rare sense of humility, which can be seen from some of the other lessons learned on this list. His appreciation of the supporting cast he has around him, as well as his ability to do what he loves for a living, factors into this development of humility.

7. Value Rest and Recovery

Durant has learned the hard way what happens when you overlook the value of rest and recovery. Although working as hard as one can is important, and has led Durant to such high levels of success, it has also led him to being sidelined. Overworking his body has led to a series of injuries. Now, however, he does a range of correctional exercises for purely preventative reasons.

8. Lead By Example

Durant has become a young leader in the NBA. Most players settle into that role in later years, but he has had to embrace it early on. The main focal point that Durant has reiterated over and over is that the greatest leader is one who leads by example. While exciting teammates and giving motivational talks can be important and useful, he believes the most important aspect of leadership is working hard, and setting the standard for the rest of your team.

9. The Game Isn't Over Until It's Over

Whether the Thunder are up by 20, down by 4, or the opposite, Durant is a firm believer in playing until the final buzzer. Basketball, a game of momentum shifts, can change quickly and dramatically. Believing that a game has been won or lost before the final seconds is something that Durant believes leads to failure.

10. Don't Forget the Joy of the Game

During points in Durant's career, usually when he is displaying anger and contempt on the court, he has forgotten the simplistic joy that has enabled him to be committed to the sport for so long. Thus, he has made a conscious effort to value the love of the game. Having fun, while it may seem somewhat irresponsible at times, is central to what Durant believes leads to success.

CHAPTER 10

DURANT'S BASKETBALL PHILOSOPHY

If Durant said his philosophy of the game in a sentence, it would probably read something like this: *"Do whatever it is you need to do to get the ball in the basket."* It sounds relatively simple, but it echoes what Durant has been able to do better than almost any basketball player, ever – get the ball in the net.

It's not just that he has already led the NBA in scoring numerous times, but it's the way that he does it. He has trained, and believes, that having the most **extensive repertoire of moves** and ways to get that ball in the hoop is what makes for truly successful players. He is precisely so impressive because he does not rely on one, or even on a small set of moves, to do what he needs to do for his team.

However, beyond scoring, Durant recognizes the need for cohesion and **teamwork** to win games. He values his teammates immensely. So much so that he looks at them as if they are family. And this is more than just genuine care. This is because he realizes that this type of unity is what wins championships.

Finally, central to Durant's philosophy of basketball is **patience**. He has had to deal with a wide range of setbacks – in his early life he dealt with poverty and a range of family issues. In his basketball career he has dealt with doubters, injuries, and everything in between. Recognizing that the path to greatness is gradual, and that years and experiences build upon each other, is central to his philosophy in life and in basketball. And the two are never mutually exclusive.

CHAPTER 11

12 INTERESTING FACTS YOU DIDN'T KNOW ABOUT KEVIN DURANT

1. Durant's emotional MVP speech was well delivered, however, he actually didn't practice. On a piece of paper before going onstage, he wrote: "Mom. Teammates." Then he wrote a few other bullet points: Russell. Scott Brooks. The Media. The fans.

2. In press conferences, Durant has always stood out. And it's not for his long lanky frame. He almost always carried a backpack, unlike other players. Many have speculated as to what is in the bag. As it turns out, it always contains a Bible, iPad, headphones and a Phone Charger.

3. In an interview with Jimmy Fallon, he got Durant talking about his enjoyment playing video games. Fallon asked Durant who he plays with; more specifically, if he plays as himself. He said no, as that would not be very humble. After some probing he admitted to playing with LeBron James the most often.

4. Growing up, Durant has said that if he was unable to get a career in basketball, he would have wanted to be a meteorologist.

5. His dream growing up was to play for the Toronto Raptors.

6. After Durant got a massive back tattoo last year, he posted an image of it onto social media. However, there was a typo. The word 'mature' was misspelled as 'mautre.' The tattoo was eventually corrected, when Durant posted another picture onto Instagram with the word 'mature' spelt correctly. Needless to say, it generated a lot of media attention.

7. Durant's favorite food is Crab Legs.

8. He has said that if he had an individual theme song to which he could walk out at games it would be "Im good" by Clipse.

9. His favorite movie is *Big Momma's House.*

10. He has a Wingspan of 7'4

11. Kevin Durant is the youngest player in the *50-40-90 Club.* Since the 1979-1980 season, only six players have shot 50 percent from the field, 40 percent from beyond the arc and 90 percent at the charity stripe for an entire NBA season.

12. He wants to be a music producer when his NBA career is done.

CHAPTER 12

AWARDS AND RECOGNITION

2015-2016

- NBA All Star
- All-NBA 2nd Team
- USA Basketball Male Athlete of the Year

2014-2015

- NBA All Star

2013-2014

- All-NBA 1st Team
- NBA MVP
- NBA Scoring Champion
- NBA All Star

2012-2013

- All-NBA 1st Team
- NBA All Star

2011-2012

- All-NBA 1st Team
- NBA Scoring Champion
- NBA All-Star Game MVP
- Olympic Gold Medal
- NBA All Star

2010-2011

- All-NBA 1st Team
- NBA Scoring Champion

- NBA All Star

2009-2010

- All-NBA 1st Team
- NBA Scoring Champion
- NBA All-Star Weekend H-O-R-S-E Competition winner
- FIBA Gold Medalist
- FIBA MVP
- NBA All Star

2008-2009

- NBA All-Star Weekend H-O-R-S-E Competition winner
- NBA Rookie Challenge MVP

2007-2008

- NBA Rookie of the Year
- All-Rookie First Team

2006-2007

- Naismith College Player of the Year
- NABC Division I Player of the Year
- AP Player of the Year
- AP All-America 1st Team
- Oscar Robertson Trophy
- Adolph Rupp Trophy
- John R. Wooden Award
- Bug 12 Player of the Year
- USBWA National Freshman of the Year

CHAPTER 13

NBA SEASON STATS

Legend					
GP	Games played	GS	Games started	MPG	Minutes per game
FG%	Field goal percentage	3P%	3-point field goal percentage	FT%	Free throw percentage
RPG	Rebounds per game	APG	Assists per game	SPG	Steals per game
BPG	Blocks per game	PPG	Points per game	Bold	Career high

†	Denotes season in which Durant won an NBA championship
*	Led the league

Regular season

Year ⬥	Team ⬥	GP ⬥	GS ⬥	MPG ⬥	FG% ⬥	3P% ⬥	FT% ⬥	RPG ⬥	APG ⬥	SPG ⬥	BPG ⬥	PPG ⬥
2007–08	Seattle	80	80	34.6	.430	.288	.873	4.4	2.4	1.0	.9	20.3
2008–09	Oklahoma City	74	74	39.0	.476	**.422**	.863	6.5	2.8	1.3	.7	25.3
2009–10	Oklahoma City	82	82	**39.5**	.476	.365	.900	7.6	2.8	**1.4**	1.0	30.1*
2010–11	Oklahoma City	78	78	38.9	.462	.350	.880	6.8	2.7	1.1	1.0	27.7*
2011–12	Oklahoma City	66	66	38.6	.496	.387	.860	8.0	3.5	1.3	1.2	28.0*
2012–13	Oklahoma City	81	81	38.5	.510	.416	**.905***	7.9	4.6	**1.4**	1.3	28.1
2013–14	Oklahoma City	81	81	38.5	.503	.391	.873	7.4	**5.5**	1.3	.7	**32.0***
2014–15	Oklahoma City	27	27	33.8	.510	.403	.854	6.6	4.1	.9	.9	25.4
2015–16	Oklahoma City	72	72	35.8	.505	.388	.898	8.2	5.0	1.0	1.2	28.2
2016–17†	Golden State	62	62	33.4	**.537**	.375	.875	**8.3**	4.9	1.1	**1.6**	25.1
Career		703	703	37.4	.488	.379	.882	7.2	3.8	1.2	1.0	27.2
All-Star		7	5	26.7	.518	.311	.900	5.6	2.9	1.6	.3	25.6

STEVE JAMES

Playoffs

Year	Team	GP	GS	MPG	FG%	3P%	FT%	RPG	APG	SPG	BPG	PPG
2010	Oklahoma City	6	6	38.5	.350	.286	.871	7.7	2.3	.5	1.3	25.0
2011	Oklahoma City	17	17	42.5	.449	.339	.838	8.2	2.8	.9	1.1	28.6
2012	Oklahoma City	20	20	41.9	.517	.373	.864	7.4	3.7	1.5	1.2	28.5
2013	Oklahoma City	11	11	44.1	.455	.314	.830	9.0	6.3	1.3	1.1	30.8
2014	Oklahoma City	19	19	42.9	.460	.344	.810	8.9	3.9	1.0	1.3	29.6
2016	Oklahoma City	18	18	40.3	.430	.282	.890	7.1	3.3	1.0	1.0	28.4
2017†	Golden State	15	15	35.5	.556	.442	.893	8.0	4.3	.8	1.3	28.5
	Career	106	106	41.0	.468	.344	.853	8.0	3.8	1.0	1.2	28.8

CONCLUSION

Kevin Durant has done more than entertain people by playing basketball. He has created a new and interesting persona that is rarely seen in professional sports. He is kind, humble, and delivers.

If he can stay healthy, Durant should have a long a promising career ahead of him. He has the potential to be one of the best and unique players in history.

Further, even when he retires, he has the potential to make a significant difference off the court. With various initiatives, charities, and business plans, Durant is going to be someone whom America does not soon forget.

ABOUT THE AUTHOR

Steve James isn't your typical sports fan. While there are some that will always make time to watch the big game, James started following the NBA at a very young age and has watched some of the best players in the history of the NBA from the very beginning. Even at that young age, he started paying attention to who was really standing out on the court–greats like Michael Jordan, Magic Johnson or Larry Bird. Steve follows the game till this date and knows the ins and outs of the greatest NBA stars of today, like Kobe Bryant, LeBron James, Kevin Durant or Stephen Curry. Having carefully watched these players on the court and studied their lives, he has a unique perspective into their success, how it was achieved, and what makes them so great.

He has an insider view into the secrets that have made these players so successful. By collecting this information into his books, he hopes to help not just young, aspiring basketball players, but all people to learn the secrets of what it takes to be successful. By looking at how these players have reached their goals, the readers will glean the information they need to reach their own goals. Steve's years of analyzing play styles, successes, failures, training routines, etc. gives him a real insight into these players!

Printed in Great Britain
by Amazon